THE SOUTH
20TH CENTURY AND
BEYOND

THE SOUTH
20TH CENTURY AND BEYOND
50 ESSENTIAL BOOKS

Clyde N. Wilson

SOUTHERN READER'S GUIDE IV

SHOTWELL PUBLISHING

Columbia, SC

THE SOUTH 20TH CENTURY AND BEYOND: 50 ESSENTIAL BOOKS

Copyright © 2021 by Clyde N. Wilson

ALL RIGHTS RESERVED. No part of this publication may be reproduced, distributed, or transmitted in any form or by any means, including photocopying, recording, or other electronic or mechanical methods, or by any information storage and retrieval system without the prior written permission of the publisher, except in the case of very brief quotations embodied in critical reviews and certain other non-commercial uses permitted by copyright law.

Produced in the Republic of South Carolina by

Shotwell Publishing, LLC
Post Office Box 2592
Columbia, South Carolina 29202

www.ShotwellPublishing.com

Covert Images: Zora Hurston, Richard Weaver, William Faulkner, & Tom Wolfe

Cover Design: Hazel's Dream | Boo Jackson TCB

ISBN: 978-1-947660-48-9

10 9 8 7 6 5 4 3 2 1

Dedicated to the Red Shirt Reading Circle

The South is a garden. It has been worn out by the War, Reconstruction, the Period of Desolation, the Depression and the worst ravages of all—Modernity; yet, a worn-out garden, its contours perceived by keen eyes, the fruitfulness of its past stored in memory, can be over time, a time which will last no longer than those of us who initially set our minds to the task, restored, to once again produce, for the time appointed unto it, the fruits which nurture the human spirit and which foreshadow the Garden of which there will be no end.
— Dr Robert M. Peters of Louisiana

I believe that the American South, the last bastion of Christianity in the West, will have a special role in the final chapter of history.
— Anne Wilson Smith

How can the traditional society be preserved as the model of the right conduct of mind in the face of the modern shift to the vision of mind as the proper model of society? This may only be accomplished, to be sure, by mind's assertion that society is its model.

— Lewis P. Simpson

Preface

THE PERIOD OF SOUTHERN WRITING covered here is a long one—most of the 20th century and up to the present day. During this era the South has existed as what the historian Charles P. Roland has called "not quite a nation within a nation, but the next thing to it." We Southerners have also played, most of the time, the role of what sociologists call "the internal other"—the unloved red-headed stepchild who is pointed to as guilty of whatever may be bad or amiss.

What strikes me most about Southern writing in this period is the way Southerners, as outsiders, have been able to diagnose the failings of America with the insight that only outsiders can have. Northerners are not noted for their sense of humour, and, unlike Southerners, are especially quite reluctant to laugh at themselves. American humour, like American music, literature, and cuisine, seems largely a Southern phenomenon. Writers like Flannery O'Connor, Tom Wolfe, Florence King, and George Garrett have been able to see the American mainstream in uncomplimentary ways that are at the same time penetrating, original, and funny.

In the beginning of his *A Disquisition on Government*, John C. Calhoun observed that society is a God-given necessity of man's nature, while governments, though necessary for the protection of society, are merely creations of men. In insisting that society precedes government, Calhoun was making explicit a Southern tradition of thought that had marked Jefferson and Taylor of Caroline, and was to mark the Confederacy, the Populists and the Agrarians. The South has valued incarnate America while its enemies have gloried in an imagined theoretical America which is to be established by government coercion of society. As the brilliant Tom Landess pointed out, our Creator communicated with us by incarnation, not theory. Here may be a key to the greatness of Southern literature. That greatness is not an anomaly or an accident but the voice of the South.

Because so many of the great Southern writers of this period have excelled in more than one form of literature—like Garrett, Wendell Berry, Robert Penn Warren, and Fred Chappell—I have tried to account for this and help the reader by choosing one major title and adding information within that entry about others that should be pursued.

The writers catalogued here, and they are only a sample, prove beyond a doubt that the South is real, that it has contributed much of value to the world, and that we are right to take our stand.

Clyde N. Wilson
Dutch Fork, South Carolina

1.

I'll Take My Stand:
The South and the Agrarian Tradition (1930)
by Twelve Southerners

MORE THAN THREE-QUARTERS of a century after it was published, *I'll Take My Stand* is still read and discussed. Part of this attention rests on the subsequent literary fame of some of the Twelve Southerners—Robert Penn Warren, John Crowe Ransom, Allen Tate, Andrew Lytle, Stark Young, and Donald Davidson. Also, on the fact that its message has been found to be of great value to many people beyond the South. But it is, as the title makes clear, about and in defense of the South as a way of thinking and living. The occasion for the book was the Great Depression and the intellectual battle between capitalism and socialism that ensued. For the Agrarians, corporate capitalism (Big Business) as it existed in America and socialism were two sides of the same centralised and inhumane coin. Their symposium was made as an argument against what they called "industrialism," by which they meant distant economic control, an unconsidered pursuit of Bigness for its own sake, materialism, and mass culture. "Industrialism" had curtailed personal freedom, commodified labour, torn people from their roots, and brought about an adulterated and artificial mass culture in place of the high culture and folk culture characteristic of a good society.

The traditional South, the Twelve Southerners maintained, still contained the material of a third way that was hardly being discussed. The writers illuminated this in regard to education, religion, literature, economics, and daily living. In the big picture, *I'll Take My Stand* was not successful but it is still strong in the hearts and minds of men and still essential in understanding what we mean by "the South."

2.
Who Owns America?
A New Declaration of Independence (1936),
edited by Herbert Agar and Allen Tate

IN *WHO OWNS AMERICA?* eight of the Twelve Southerners of *I'll Take My Stand* were joined by other Southern, Northern, and British writers in the battle against the twins Big Business and Socialism. We find persuasive arguments against the remote, impersonal irresponsibility of the giant corporation, the end of the widespread ownership of productive property that constitutes a good and free society, the false ideal of gigantism in institutions, the exploitation of women as industrial labour in the guise of "emancipation," and the destruction of faith being carried out by "liberal Protestantism." We might say that *Who Owns America?* is a reformulation of the South's Jeffersonian democracy and economics for a new and very different age. The Texas historian Walter Prescott Webb made the case again in *Divided We Stand: The Crisis of a Frontierless Democracy* (1937), describing the South and West as exploited colonies of Northern capital.

3.
Southern By the Grace of God
by Michael Andrew Grissom

OKLAHOMAN MICHAEL GRISSOM'S best-selling classic has been called "a moving journey into the heart and soul of the South. It captures the emotional and very human essence of Southern culture . . . ." A heart-warming celebration for those who have receptive hearts. Enough said.

4.
Confederaphobia: An American Epidemic
by Paul C. Graham

THROUGH MOST OF THE 20TH century Americans lived in peace with the memory of the vast bloodletting revolution of the War Between the States. It was agreed that the war was a great tragedy with good and bad on both sides. Southerners were glad that the Union had been preserved. Northerners were willing to acknowledge that Confederates had been brave and sincere and that Confederate heroes like Lee and Jackson were great

Americans. Southern soldiers displayed Confederate flags in World War II and Korea and later. U.S. Presidents were not ashamed to be seen with Confederate flags and to praise Robert E. Lee. From late in the last century up to the present time, public discussion has manifested an intense hatred of everything Confederate. Public life is now dominated by the claim that the Confederacy is the seat of all evil in American history and that therefore all its symbols should be obliterated. The rise of this hatred dates from the collapse of the Civil Rights movement after its success against discrimination and its change into a vested interest eager to keep alive a rewarding status of victimhood. Also, from the penetration of Cultural Marxism into the dominant organs of American society. Graham has aptly dubbed this malady "Confederaphobia," catalogued the truly absurd behaviour exhibited by those affected, and diagnosed its causes.

5.
The Time of Man (1926)
by Elizabeth Madox Roberts

ELIZABETH MADOX ROBERTS (1881 - 1941) of Kentucky is certainly one of the greatest of Southern women writers—although the competition is stiff. To say the greatest Southern woman writer of course means the same thing as the greatest American woman writer. Roberts's powerful prose is an inimitable combination of realism and lyric beauty. In *The Old South: 50 Essential Books* we listed *The Great Meadow*, her book about the early settlement of Kentucky. It is not easy to make a choice of one out of her works set in later times. *The Time of Man* is a moving story of the poorest class of white Southerners in the 1920s wresting a living from the land, a true rendering of a phase of Southern life that is not long past. (See *The Old South: 50 Essential Books*, No. 16.)

6.
Go Down Moses by William Falkner

AMONG ALL THE PRODUCTS of Faulkner's genius, this work covers a long period of time—mid-19th century through early 20th century—in the lives of white, black, and red Mississippians. The book is sometimes considered as a collection of stories, and indeed one section, "The Bear," is sometimes separately printed. But the unity becomes apparent when you understand that the main character is not a person but the community—Yoknapatawpha County itself. Outside critics have often considered Ike McCaslin to be a hero because he rejected his inheritance tainted by slavery. But that is not Faulkner's intention. Ike is a failure, a barren abstractionist. It is his worldly cousin Cass Edmonds who takes responsibility for what is and the people around him despite the bad history and troubled moral situation. If, as you should, you want to read more Faulkner, I suggest, in this order, *The Unvanquished*, *Intruder in the Dust*, and the Snopes trilogy: *The Hamlet*, *The Town*, and *The Mansion*. For understanding Faulkner see *William Faulkner: Yoknapatawpha Country* by Cleanth Brooks. For Faulkner speaking as himself, a conservative Southerner, see *Essays, Speeches and Public Letters* by William Faulkner, edited by James B. Meriwether. (See below Nos. 42 and 46.)

7.
Aleck Maury, Sportsman (1934)
by Caroline Gordon

THIS INNOCUOUSLY TITLED work is a true classic. It has won great praise as a perfectly crafted novel and for its portrayal of a Southern life. Aleck Maury's job was a teacher of classics. His life was hunting and fishing. Andrew Lytle wrote of this book: "It is, in a sense, a prose *Aeneid*, written with so much economy and constraint that the reader is only aware at the end that he has been following the wonderings of a hero." Caroline Gordon (1895 - 1981) is one of those great Southern women writers who is known but not as well-known as she should be. You will doubtless want to read more. Go to her War Between the States novel *None Shall Look Back*, her novel of the Tennessee frontier *Green Centuries*, and *The Collected Stories of Caroline Gordon*.

8.
Their Eyes Were Watching God
by Zora Neale Hurston

ZORA NEALE HURSTON (1891 - 1960) was the greatest African American writer yet produced in the U.S. and has a place in the distinguished company of outstanding Southern writers of the 20th century. The proof is in the high quality of her prolific work and perhaps in the criticism and obstruction she endured from other African American writers. Hurston grew up in an all-black town in Florida, which is the fictionalised scene of much of her work. *Their Eyes Were Watching God* is a moving story of a woman's search for love in a world of cruel and indifferent men. Among other virtues it provides the reader with a sympathetic view of the interior life of a black community that can teach us much. Hurston was a novelist and not a political crusader and she drew on the same deep wells of Southern culture that Faulkner and others drew on. (The movie version of *Their Eyes Were Watching God* is faithful to the story, but is spoiled because the central character is played by a half-white actress with Anglo-Saxon features. Hurston and her character were black and proud of it.) This is one of those books that makes you want more of the author. Move on to her non-fiction *Mules and Men*, her autobiography *Dust Tracks on a Road*. For those who want a realistic picture of American slavery, get Hurston's *Bacaroon*.

9.
Punished with Poverty:
The Suffering South - Prosperity to Poverty and the Continuing Struggle
by James Ronald Kennedy and Walter Donald Kennedy

"IT IS TRUE WE are completely under the saddle of Massachusetts and Connecticut," wrote Thomas Jefferson in 1798, "and that they ride us very hard, cruelly insulting our feelings, as well as exhausting our strength and substance." Jefferson was asking whether joining New England in the United States had not become a bad bargain for the South. Through the colonial period and into the early 19th century, the South was very prosperous. Since then, with tariffs and North-favouring expenditures, destruction by invasion, Reconstruction looting, and partial legislation, Southerners, black and white, have been, and still are, up to the present moment, the poorest Americans—and Southern "feelings" suffer from constant denunciation for being out-of-step in religion and values from the rest of the U.S. The Kennedy brothers, long known as fearless spokesmen for the Southern people, have written an original and important contribution to Southern history. They relate the long story of the poverty imposed on the South. They wonder why Southerners are not more conscious of their inferior position in "America," and they propose unconventional political action to do something about it. *Punished with Poverty* is followed by *Dixie Rising*, a handbook for that political action.

10.
The Southern Diaspora: How the Great Migration of Black and White Southerners Transformed America
by James N. Gregory

FROM 1900 TO 1970 SOME 20 million Southerners, black and white, left home for the North and West. Mostly driven by need, for who would willingly leave the South? Much has been written about the black migration of 8 million, but the white movement was considerably larger if not as noticeable. These numbers make a mass migration of world historical dimensions. Professor Gregory has done a good job of telling the history of this migration and also of the important changes that Southerners in their migration have made to American society in the regions to which they have gone. This is a very large matter in the long experience of the Southern people that has not been noticed nearly enough and the consequences of which are still unfolding. For instance, much has been made of the behaviour of working-class Democrats in the "Rust Belt" in the 2016 Presidential election, but few have noticed how much this depended on the Southern base of much of the population.

11.

The Dollmaker by Harriette Arnow

THE DOLLMAKER IS the story of a Kentucky country woman. Need drives her and her family to the alien land of industrial Detroit. Arnow has portrayed movingly a neglected phase of Southern history—the millions of Southerners, white and black, who in a great 20th century diaspora migrated to the North and West. I am not much of a sentimentalist, but *The Dollmaker*, in portraying the travails of our people, brought me as close to tears as any book I have read. Except perhaps Shelby Foote's account of the third day at Gettysburg. The movie version of "The Dollmaker," starring Jane Fonda, believe it or not, is pretty good.

12.

Country Music, U.S.A. by Bill C. Monroe

THIS IS A THOROUGH AND lively history of the Southern artistry, "country" music, that captured the world—until its heart and soul were ruined by New York executives and music videos. The first edition was published in 1968. The most recent, 2010, brings the story up to less interesting recent times.

13.
Ideas Have Consequences (1948) by Richard M. Weaver

IDEAS HAVE CONSEQUENCES by the North Carolinian Richard M. Weaver may be considered a gift of the South to the world. It is a philosophical examination of "the ills of our age" and "the sickness of modern culture." This book was a major document in the rise of American intellectual conservatism in the post-World War II era, until that movement was co-opted under Ronald Reagan by the Trotskyite apparatchiks known as Neoconservatives. The work was widely praised in its time, although many of its admirers probably did not realize that it could only have been written by a thinker from the Southern culture. It is perhaps not too much to affirm that nobody can really understand the world we live in today, so well and prophetically diagnosed by Weaver, without Weaver's wisdom. Weaver (1910 - 1963) received the doctorate under Cleanth Brooks at Louisiana State University and taught for many years at the University of Chicago. In summers he went home to North Carolina to work on the family farm.

14.

The Southern Essays of Richard M. Weaver

WEAVER THOUGHT THAT the South was "the last non-materialist civilization" in the Western world. Southerners had held onto many of the old inherited and once taken-for-granted ways of the West in regard to religion, chivalry, and community, in a time dominated by materialist assumptions, goals and mass culture. This collection includes essays on Southern literature, on Southern history, and on "The Southern Tradition for an American Future." Weaver is always penetrating and original, but especially important perhaps is "Two Types of American Individualism." In this piece he makes the vital distinction between the "social bond individualism" that governs community in the South and the collectivist, top-down version of community of the North. This work is but a small sample of Weaver. Follow up with the Weaver collections *Visions of Order*, and *In Defense of Tradition* edited by Ted J. Smith, III.

15.

Home by the River (1941) by Archibald Rutledge

ARCHIBALD RUTLEDGE (1883 - 1973) was in his time the very popular author of over 50 books, many about hunting and fishing or involving gentle views of living like an early (1928) work, *Life's Extras*. The "home" is the colonial family plantation in Low Country of South Carolina. On retirement he returned "home" to live fulltime and preserve and maintain the place. You will want to be sure to read Rutledge's "My Colonel and His Lady" and to enjoy his unsurpassed knowledge of the natural world of his region.

16.
The Old Man and the Boy (1957)
by Robert C. Ruark

ROBERT CHESTER RUARK (1915 - 1965) of North Carolina was famous in his time. A prodigy, he entered the University of North Carolina at 15. After service as a merchant seaman and a combat Navy officer in World War II, he became a well-known, world-traveled journalist, columnist, and author—also acquiring a reputation as a big game hunter in Africa. His best known works are his two novels about the Mau Mau uprising in Kenya: *Something of Value* (made into a big star movie) and *Uhuru!* In *The Old Man and the Boy*, which is somewhat autobiographical, he tells the story of a boy initiated by his grandfather into hunting and fishing (and life) in the game-rich coastal area of North Carolina near Wilmington. This is a wonderful portrayal of a long-lasting aspect of Southern life. *The Old Man's Boy Grows Older* is a sequel. Ruark spent his last years living in Spain—at the same time as another famous North Carolinian. Can you guess who? [rendraG avA]

17.

Lee in the Mountains and Other Poems (1949) by Donald Davidson

DAVIDSON WAS THE MOST faithful of the Southern Agrarians, never ceasing to be a spokesman for the Southern tradition in essays, literary criticism, history, and especially poetry. There are other more comprehensive collections of Davidson's poetry, but this edition celebrates in unforgettable verse the life and heroism of our frontier and Confederate forebears and probes the conflicted souls of "modern" Southerners. I found a tattered copy of this book in the back room of a bookstore over 50 years ago. It remains on my nearest shelf next to the Bible and the old Prayer Book. For Davidson's prose see *Southern Writers in the Modern World*; *Attack on Leviathan*; *Still Rebels, Still Yankees*; and his two-volume history of the Tennessee River valley.

18.
Generations of the Faithful Heart: On the Literature of the South
by M.E. Bradford

WITH THE PASSING OF MOST of the Agrarian writers and Richard Weaver, it was thought that the Southern intellectual tradition was moribund. The brilliant Southwesterner M.E. Bradford, a student of Donald Davidson at Vanderbilt, proved this wrong. He not only defended the South from high ground, he expanded the reach and relevance of its thought into new and wider areas. Among other accomplishments, Bradford shed new light on Lincoln, on the American Revolution and Constitution, and on contemporary events. His earliest scholarship was on literature. This book concerns the Southernness of Southern writers: Eudora Welty, Robert Penn Warren, John Crowe Ransom, Caroline Gordon, Walker Percy, and especially William Faulkner. The book's title is taken from a line of Davidson's great poem "Lee in the Mountains." For more of Bradford see *The Old South: 50 Essential Books*, No. 11, and *A Defender of Southern Conservatism: M.E. Bradford and His Achievements*, edited by Clyde N. Wilson. (See also No. 50 below.)

19.
All the Brave Promises . . .
by Mary Lee Settle

MARY LEE SETTLE (1918 - 2005) is one of those writers who is well-known but not as well-known as they should be. She was born Charleston, West Virginia. As a young woman she was a model and actress in New York and was actually screen-tested for the part of Scarlett O'Hara in "Gone with the Wind." She is best known for her Beulah Quintet, five novels portraying the history of West Virginia from the beginning to well into the 20th century: *Prisons, O Beulah Land, Know Nothing, The Scapegoat,* and *The Killing Ground*. I have chosen to bring to attention this gripping memoir of a Southerner in World War II. Settle went to Britain before Pearl Harbor and joined the Women's Auxiliary Air Force. She worked as a radio operator in communication with pilots in the air on dangerous missions. This is her story. The book's subtitle is *Memories of Aircraft Woman 2nd Class 2146391.*

20.
With the Old Breed: At Peleliu and Okinawa
by Eugene B. Sledge

THAT VAST EVENT CALLED World War II absorbed and changed the lives of millions of Southerners as it did many other peoples. Eugene Sledge, a young Alabamian, served through the fierce combat of the Pacific in the 1st Marine Division (the "Old Breed"). His memoir is based on notes he kept in the margins of his New Testament during his service. *With the Old Breed* has become a popular resource for treating World World War II experiences. For instance, Sledge is a character in the television series "The Pacific." The book is more than a war journal, however. It is also a spiritual experience—from hate and horror to healing. Sledge became a popular science professor at Auburn University. (In one edition there is an irrelevant Introduction by the absurdly over-rated historian V.D. Hanson, which can be safely ignored.) For a very small sampling of Southern contributions to World War II, look up Simon B. Buckner Jr., Nathan Bedford Forrest III, Audie Murphy, Chester W. Nimitz, George S. Patton, and "Chesty" Puller.

21.
The Emergence of the New South, 1913 – 1945
by George B. Tindall

TINDALL WAS A NATIVE OF South Carolina and a long-time professor at the University of North Carolina. This straightforward and even-handed work offers a good survey of the period it covers.

22.

The Enduring South:
Subcultural Persistence in Mass Society
by John Shelton Reed

REED, A LONG-TIME PROFESSOR of sociology at the University of North Carolina, is a sociologist who writes like a humane man of letters. He uses a large variety of statistics to plot the differences between Southerners and other Americans. The differences are real: in religious orthodoxy, in family and local orientation, in certain attitudes toward government and the uses of violence. The conclusion: Southerners are different and likely to stay that way. The book was first published in 1972 and updated with data from the 1980s that did not alter the conclusion.

23.

The Burden of Brown:
Thirty Years of School Desegregation
by Raymond Wolters

THE 1954 BROWN V. BOARD of Education decision of the U.S. Supreme Court was the starting point of immense changes in Southern, and American, society. Wolters, Professor of History at the University of Delaware, tells the history straightforwardly and factually, without sentimentality, of how the decision came about and its effects.

24.
Flannery O'Connor: Collected Works, edited by Sally Fitzgerald

FLANNERY O'CONNOR OF Georgia is widely considered to have been one of the most important American writers of our time. Her fiction is filled with odd and often sinister characters and events that have been called "grotesque." For O'Connor her characters were not grotesque but only seemed so to people who had entirely forgotten about Original Sin. They were not merely exhibits of Southern depravity—the author remarked that Yankees would believe anything about the South if it were strange enough. Rather, the stories were observations from a deeply Christian perspective of times and people devoid of all "spiritual purpose." You have to be extreme to reach such empty and hard-headed people, she said. Her fiction reflected the world as seen through Christian commitment and Southern imagination. This is an excellent collection, including O'Connor's novels, some short stories, and a generous collection of her essays and letters, which are as important as her fiction. O'Connor thought that outsiders were mistaken in believing that the South suffered from being alien to the American mainstream; rather, the South suffered from not being alien enough.

25.
A Texan Looks at Lyndon:
A Study in Illegitimate Power (1964)
by J. Evetts Haley

THIS BOOK IS SAID TO have sold 7.5 million copies during the 1964 presidential campaign, making it one of the political best-sellers of all time. Texas cattleman, politician, and historian Haley traces the dubious career of "Landslide Lyndon" from the dirt up to the White House. Haley had observed Texas politics closely for a long time and knew what he was saying. The book is more than a document for one occasion. It allows us to review, sadly, the corruption that has marked so much of 20th century Southern politics, especially since the "Great Society."

26.
Chronicles of the South (2 vols.),
edited by Clyde N. Wilson

CHRONICLES: A MAGAZINE of American Culture, although published in the Midwest, was, unlike most national publications, friendly to Southern writers and Southern subjects during its heyday under the editorship of Thomas Fleming. These two volumes collect material that appeared in the journal over several decades. Vol. 1 is *Garden of the Beaux Arts* and focuses on Southern literature. There are outstanding pieces by and about such writers as Andrew

Lytle, George Garrett, M.E. Bradford, Walker Percy, Donald Davidson, Fred Chappell, Thomas Landess, Mark Royden Winchell, Egon Tausch, and others. Vol. 2, *In Justice to So Fine a Country*, focuses on larger issues of Southern history, culture, and current affairs. It includes pieces by Donald Livingston, J.O. Tate, John Shelton Reed, Jack Trotter, Garrett, Landess, and others.

27.
The Burning Fields: Poems and Beyond the Chandeleurs: Poems by David Middleton

THE LOUISIANA POET David Middleton has cast everyday Southern life into memorable form in his verse. Rarer than most poets, he also conveys a broad historical and religious vision from a Southern and Christian viewpoint. Middleton's work will grow more important as the New South works itself through time. Continue on with the recent *The Fiddler of Driskill Hill*.

28.
I Am One of Your Forever by Fred Chappell

FRED CHAPPELL of North Carolina is one of those Southern men of letters (like Poe, Simms, Warren, Berry, Garrett) who excels in multiple types of literature. He is best-known and most honoured as a poet. His accomplishments are also outstanding in fiction, essays, and translation of poetry from the ancient classics. The novel *I Am One of You Forever* is the beautiful account of a North Carolina mountain family, their kin and neighbours, on the eve of World War II. Chappell writes here with an inimitable combination of realism and sentiment laced with exhilarating touches of Southern tall tale. This work's characters are followed further in *Brighten the Corner Where You Are*; *Farewell, I'm Bound to Leave You*; and *Look Back All the Green Valley*.

29.
Lost in the Cosmos: The Last Self-Help Book
(1983) by Walker Percy

LOUISIANAN WALKER PERCY (1916 - 1990) achieved greatest fame for his novels like *The Moviegoer*, *Love in the Ruins*, *The Second Coming*, and others.

These are stories about the lives of Southerners in "modern" times, but they are much more than that. They are explorations of the crisis of human identity in those same times from the loss of civlisation and Christianity. The deterioration of American society is viewed in a way that can only be the product of a Southern sensibility. In his nonfiction *Lost in the Cosmos* Percy approaches his theme by philosophical speculation. Serious reading.

30.
What Are People For?
Essays by Wendell Berry

WENDELL BERRY OF Kentucky is one of those supreme men of letters that only the South produces in America. He is equally excellent in poetry, fiction, and essays—like Poe and Simms in earlier times and like his contemporaries Robert Penn Warren, George Garrett, and Fred Chappell. Among other accomplishments Berry has become perhaps the most recognised American spokesman for environmental care, sustainable agriculture, local economy, and old-fashioned ways, in contrast to the haste, waste, injustice, and imperialsim of industrial America. These essays are perhaps the best first approach to the breadth and depth of Berry's wisdom, which may be considered a continuation of the message of the Agrarian writers of *I'll Take My Stand*. Berry's poetry and fiction are so rich that one hardly knows where to start recommending. You can go wrong with nothing from his pen. For fiction start with *Jayber Crow* and *The Memory of Old Jack*, *A Place on Earth*, and *That Distant Land*. His verse appears in *Selected Poems* and *Collected Poems of Wendell Berry*.

31.
If I Ever Get Back to Georgia I'm Gonna Nail My Feet to the Ground
by Lewis Grizzard

THE ATLANTA COLUMNIST Lewis Grizzard (1946 - 1994) was an inimitable and hilarious expositor of the popular culture and unreconstructed sentiment of the South in his time. His material appeared in over 30 books and there are several extant multi-volume collections. Reading Grizzard is always a refreshing and joyful encounter for any Southerner. I have chosen one title for the heading out of many, but all can be recommended. Try *I Haven't Understood Anything Since 1962 and Other Nekkid Truths, Elvis is Dead and I Don't Feel So Good Myself, They Tore Out My Heart and Stomped that Sucker Flat,* or any others.

32.
When the Walls Came Tumbling Down: An Autobiography (1989)
by Ralph David Abernathy

THE REV. MR. ABERNATHY (1926 - 1990) of Alabama was a major figure in the "Civil Rights" movement that looms so large in Southern and American history. He knew most of the major actors of the time. Unlike some of his colleagues, Abernathy was a genuine Christian minister and a man of broad perspective. He tells the story of important events not as dry history or as self-righteous harangue but in a personal and engaging way. He writes usually very candidly and with genuine historical perspective, although it is established that the publisher refused to make public all that he had to say about Martin Luther King, Jr. It is worth noting that the Southern Agrarian Thomas H. Landess collaborated with Abernathy on the writing of this memoir. (See below No. 48.)

33.
Poems from Scorched Earth
by James Everett Kibler

SOUTH CAROLINIAN KIBLER is a major scholar of Southern literature, being, among other things, the foremost figure in bringing William Gilmore Simms back to what is now great attention (despite false statements in Wikipedia). He is also a novelist and poet. In *Poems from Scorched Earth* a Southerner laments the wounds done to human life by the loss of place and continuity that afflicts contemporary society. He relates this to the soulless abstraction and destructiveness of the 20th century, anticipated by Sherman's scorched earth in Dixie.

34.
The Yankee Problem: An American Dilemma
(2016) by Clyde N. Wilson

"YANKEE" HERE DOES NOT mean all Northern people. It refers, as the term originally did, to a particular type originating in New England and spread across the Deep North (Northeast, upper Midwest, Pacific Coast). Real Yankees are easily identifiable by their arrogance, greed, hypocrisy, penchant for ordering other people around, and assumption that America belongs to them entirely. The history of the Yankee and his destructive influence on American life is traced from its colonial beginning to the present. His continuing dominance in recent times, exhibited by such people as George W. Bush and Hillary Rodham Clinton, is closely examined. *The Yankee Problem* covers a major aspect of American history that is seldom noticed. Writing this book was fun.

35.
Talmadge: A Political Legacy, a Politician's Life by Herman E. Talmadge with Mark Royden Winchell

HERMAN TALMADGE (1913 - 2002) was twice governor of Georgia and a U.S. Senator from 1956 to 1980, one of the last influential Southern Democrats during a period of immense change in American society. His memoirs provide a valuable close-up and uncustomary perspective on Southern and U.S. events. Our work would be incomplete without a reference to Mark Royden Winchell (1948 - 2008), a very talented and prolific scholar. Winchell's work contributed great value to the understanding of Southern literature and history. His books, among many others, included biographies of two major Southern literary figures—Cleanth Brooks and Donald Davidson, insightful studies of "neoconservatism," and *God, Man, and Hollywood: Politically Incorrect Cinema from 'The Birth of a Nation' to 'The Passion of the Christ.'*

36.
The Politically Incorrect Guide to the South (And Why It Will Rise Again)
by Clint Johnson

A PLATINUM TOUR DE FORCE. The author deftly and unabashedly tells what Southerners think and how we behave—in response to the eternal malicious misunderstandings perpetrated against our ilk. A noted scholar writes, "the book is hell-raisin' fun! I guarantee that Southerners and other normal people will have a good ol' time with this high-spirited read, a soul-lifting experience unmatched since Toscanini conducted 'Dixie'."

37.
Fields of Fire by James Webb

SOUTHERNERS PLAYED a significant part in the U.S. military through much of the 20th century, although that role seems to have grown smaller as the brass have become devotees of Cultural Marxism. Jim Webb was a combat Marine officer in Vietnam. This book is about a young officer from the South. It has been called "a searing novel of the Vietnam War, a novel of poetic power, razor-sharp observation, and agonizing human truths." Perhaps Webb should have continued as a novelist rather than undertaken the somewhat quixotic political career he has followed since leaving the Corps. Then again, he may have purged what he had to say on the experience. (Obiter dicta: I do not share the widespread admiration for Webb's book on the Scots-Irish in America, *Born Fighting*. It contributes to the mistaken theory that Southern distinctiveness is primarily "Celtic." That influence was important but by no means the only ingredient in creating Southern culture. Further, Webb's exposition uses class resentment to divide up Southerners unnecessarily and inaccurately into Scots-Irish and their "oppressors." By separating the Scots-Irish from other Southerners, his book moves into the popular category of anti-Southern.)

38.
The Florence King Reader (1995)

FLORENCE KING OF VIRGINIA undoubtedly has a high place on the honour role of American humourists. This collection of her articles and columns is a fine introduction to what has been called her "acerbic" wit. King left in shreds much of American life—bad manners, flabby "niceness," intellectual shallowness. Her ability to see the defects of "normal" American life was only possible from a Southern viewpoint. Follow up with *Reflections in a Jaundiced Eye*. She once denied being obsessed with the late War Between the States. She was too busy planning for the next one, she said, a position supported by her regular visits to the firing range.

39.
Southern Excursions: Views on Southern Letters in My Time by George Garrett

NO GUIDE TO SOUTHERN (or American) literature in the 20th century can ignore George Garrett, a man of letters who excelled in fiction, poetry, essays, screenwriting and teaching. Garrett (1929 - 2008) was raised in old pre-Disney Florida and was a boxer and Army sergeant before turning to literature. His novels of Elizabethan England, *Death of the Fox* and *The Succession* are masterpieces in anybody's book. All of Garrett's works are worth attention. We have chosen this 2003 collection of his pieces on Southern books and authors and Southern life in his time, which is a good introduction to Garrett's style and viewpoint. He was a relentless and humourous critic of the literary celebrities of New York and the shortcomings of American life in books like *My Silk Purse and Yours*, *The Sorrows of Fat City*, and others. Garrett's *Poison Pen* (1986) is a hilarious satire of the superficiality and triviality of American "culture." Garrett received considerable recognition in his lifetime but not nearly enough to equal his real stature. You may look forward to getting to know the art and thought of a great Southerner. (See *The Old South: 50 Essential Books*, No. 2.)

40.
Hooking Up by Tom Wolfe

THE VIRGINIAN Tom Wolfe was for several decades a literary lion of Manhattan. He began with creative high-end journalism (the "New Journalism") as in *The Right Stuff*, about the first astronauts, and *Radical Chic* and *Mau-Mauing the Flak Catchers*, describing wealthy fashionable "revolutionaries" and racial intimidation as a form of profit-seeking. Other books exposed fakery in art and architectural fashion. A series of novels followed—*Bonfire of the Vanities*, *A Man in Full*, *I am Charlotte Simmons*, *Back to Blood*. In his novels, any of which is worthwhile and enjoyable, Wolfe tells a good story but also shows unattractive aspects of American society that are not noticed by current fashionable discourse. In *Bonfire of the Vanities*, Wolfe satirized every institution and ethnic group in New York City and was celebrated for it. (The movie version completely and probably deliberately missed the point.) It seemed strange that he was praised by the people he exposed at their worst. George Garrett explained this as a question of manners. The New York literary celebrities are so alien from the concept of manners that they did not recognise what for a Southerner would be seen as deadly insult. The New York intellectuals specialise in the avant-garde, pornography, and world-changing manifestos. Unlike Wolfe, they never notice the people around them. The North Carolinian William Sidney Porter ("O. Henry") had a relationship with NYC similar to Wolfe's in earlier times. I have picked a recent work, *Hooking Up*, as a good initiation to Wolfe. It is a collection of short pieces, fiction and nonfiction, about various aspects of our contemporary American society—including a demolition of the pretensions of television "news" and of current literary celebrities.

41.
The Hunt for Confederate Gold (2005)
by Thomas Moore

THE LAST FEW YEARS have seen a surprising number of near-future books and even series of books that portray a scenario leading to Southern independence. This is my favourite. A descendant of the young navy officer who had charge of the Confederate Treasury gold at the end of The War gets on the trail of where that treasure might be today. Meanwhile, a number of other interesting things are happening to encourage supporters of independence. Most of these books take it for granted that a "liberal" U.S. establishment is evil and bent on suppressing traditional people by persecution. Two other favourites in this category are *Heiland* by Franklin Sanders and *A Single Star* by Stan Barnett.

42.
Intruder in the Dust (1948)
by William Faulkner

FAULKNER CLEARLY INTENDED this work as a kind of commentary on present and future possibilities of relationships of white and black in Southern society. An old lady and two boys (one white, one black) undertake a risky midnight expedition to prove a somewhat cantankerous black man not guilty of a murder charge. A year after publication, the book was made into a pretty good movie.

43.

The Arrogance of Power (1966) and *The Price of Empire* (1967) by J. William Fulbright

KNOWN AND CELEBRATED as a "liberal" during the Vietnam War era, Fulbright was actually a quite independent-minded public figure. In some respects he represented a remnant of the Southern Democratic Jeffersonian tradition, and he was never anti-South. It is said that John F. Kennedy wanted Fulbright for Secretary of State but declined to nominate him because of massive criticism of his pro-South views.

James William Fulbright (1905 - 1995) was Senator from Arkansas 1945 - 1975, losing his 30-year seat because of opposition to the Vietnam War. Liberals celebrated Fulbright for that opposition, without realising that, while they opposed the war because it was anti-Communist, he opposed it because of the dread of the damage done to America by commitment to a military empire. Fulbright wrote that setting out to police the world and rescue mankind avoided dealing with internal problems and destroyed our hallowed tradition of inspiring by example. A similar position was taken by another representative of the last Southern Democrat power in national affairs.

Robert C. Byrd of West Virginia, Senator 1959 - 2010, questioned the wisdom of the Vietnam War. He vigorously opposed the U.S. expedition into Iraq, as indicated in his speeches and his 2004 book *Losing America: Confronting a Reckless and Arrogant Presidency*. Alas, by the time Byrd wrote anti-war had become a left-wing syndrome and Southern politics had been absorbed by party-first empty suit Republicans.

44.

The Southern Nation: The New Rise of the Old South (2000) by R. Gordon Thornton

THIS OVERLOOKED WORK is a brilliant consideration of the current state and future prospects of the Southern people, understood as a nation.

45.

The Education of Little Tree (1976) by "Forrest" Carter

THIS BOOK IS IMPORTANT because of what it reveals about the ignorance and shallowness of the U.S. literary establishment. For anyone who actually reads the book, it is obviously a novel and an account of the persecution of Southerners by Yankee do-gooders. However, this first-person account of the travails of a Cherokee boy was taken as an actual memoir and as ammunition in guilt-tripping the public about the mistreatment of Native Americans. It reached best-seller status, was republished in 2001 by the University of New Mexico Press as a classic of Native American studies, and given a place on Oprah Winfrey's recommended reading list. Then (shudder!!) it was discovered that the author was actually Asa Earl Carter (1925 - 1979) who was from Alabama and had been a speechwriter for George C. Wallace. Carter was also the author of *The Rebel Outlaw Josey Wales*, the basis of a major Clint Eastwood movie, and *Watch for Me on the Mountain*, an empathetic and insightful story of Native Americans. The movie version of "The Education of Little Tree" missed the point entirely, making it a story of persecution by Southern religious bigots.

46.

William Faulkner: The Essays, Speeches, and Public Letters (2005), edited by James B. Meriwether

THE IMPORTANT THING about a great author is his God-given vision and not his opinions. However, Faulkner could not avoid at times being a public figure and his greatness makes his opinions of genuine interest. These documents include the Nobel address and other important speeches, nonfiction articles, and other material which tell us about Faulkner as citizen. Faulkner's opinions on such subjects as California, commercial athletics, and other contemporary matters are of interest. Without question his view of the world identifies him as a traditional Southerner. It is little noticed, but at his death Faulkner was working on a nonfiction work to be called "The American Dream: What Happened to It?" Some finished parts of this project appear here. Clearly, Faulkner sensed decline, failure, and lost values in his American time—the dominance of comfort over liberty and a "failure of taste and responsibility" that he found in our society.

47.

Music From the Lake and Other Essays
by Catherine Savage Brosman

HERE IS YET ANOTHER of those writers who excel in so many ways that to choose one title as "essential" is arbitrary. Brosman is equally admired for scholarship, essays, and perhaps most importantly, poetry. A long-time professor at Tulane University, she is recognised on both sides of the Atlantic as a leading scholar of French literature, as well as an authority on Louisiana Creole literature and Southwestern women writers. *Music from the Lake* is a collection of graceful essays in favour of traditional literature and life as compared to our present condition. For just a beginning with the writer's rich treasury of poetry try *Watering, Places in Mind, The Range of Light,* and *On the Old Plaza,* works to savour and come back to again.

48.
Life, Literature, and Lincoln
by Thomas H. Landess

THOMAS H. LANDESS (1931 - 2012) was gifted both as a literary scholar and an insightful observer of contemporary Southern and American life. This eclectic collection provides a mere sample of his extensive writings of both kinds. A second generation Agrarian, he was acquainted with many of the authors of *I'll Take My Stand* and recounts here stories of their lives that are not elsewhere recorded. He was also a colleague and close friend of M.E. Bradford. This volume contains evaluations of Bradford's character and work, a definitive close-up account of the conspiracy that denied Bradford appointment as head of the National Endowment for the Humanities, and several highly original articles on Lincoln. (See also No. 32 above.)

49.
Yankee Empire:
Aggressive Abroad and Despotic at Home
by James Ronald Kennedy
and Walter Donald Kennedy

IN 1866, IN RESPONSE to the British historian Lord Acton, General Robert E. Lee wrote that he feared the newly consolidated national government which had replaced the old Union would likely become "aggressive abroad and despotic at home," like other such governments had too often become in history. The Kennedys, well-known for many well-recognised books examining America from a Southern viewpoint, have taken Lee's unexampled wisdom to heart. In a historical survey that is startlingly relevant to today, they trace the history of American imperialism. The conquest of the South for the benefit of state capitalism is the first exhibit. American imperialism continued with the illegal annexation of Hawaii, the brutal suppression of Philippine independence, and armed interventions in the Caribbean and South America—all, like the conquest of the South, motivated by greed but covered by a pretense of doing good to people less enlightened than the Yankee. (The Republican party platform of 1900 avowed that the Filipinos should be crushed for resisting, like the Southern rebels, the benefits bestowed by the greatest government on earth.) Any American who is concerned about the worldwide military empire of the U.S. today will profit greatly from this eloquent and hard-hitting work.

50.

Remembering Who We Are: Observations of a Southern Conservative by M.E. Bradford

BRADFORD'S VARIED discussions of the meaning of being Southern and the relation of that identity to the present world will give much food for thought for those later "generations of the faithful heart." It is a good place for us to conclude my suggestions. (See No. 18 above and *The Old South: 50 Essential Books*, No. 11.)

Obiter Dicta

As always we welcome suggestions of good things we have missed. We have tried to account for the most important authors of and about the South in the time period covered. An obvious omission is Robert Penn Warren, from whose huge corpus I did not find any single item I wished to make stand out. Another omission is James Lee Burke, whose 22 (so far) novels about Detective Dave Robicheaux rise above the crime fiction genre and have won him recognition as one of America's outstanding writers. He has created in fiction an entire realistic world of memorable characters in the dark side of modern New Orleans and South Louisiana.

And a Few More

Here are 100 more 20th – 21st century Southern books, that have not been features as Essential Books in Southern Reader's Guides 1 - 4, but are worthy of any Southern bookshelf.

Abbeville Institute Scholars, *Exploring the Southern Tradition*

Macdonald King Aston, *Yankee Babylon*

Mark Atkins, *Women in Combat*

Stan Barnett, *A Single Star*

Joyce Bennett, *Maryland, My Maryland: The Cultural Cleansing of a Small Southern State*

Wendell Berry, *Collected Poems, Jayber Crow*

M.E. Bradford, *Against the Barbarians, The Reactionary Imperative*

Jerry C. Brewer, *Dismantling the Republic*

Cleanth Brooks, *William Faulkner: Yoknapatawpha Country*

Boyd Cathey, *The Land We Love*

Fred Chappell, *Midquest*

H. Lee Cheek, *Calhoun and Majority Rule*

Oliver P. Chitwood and Frank L. Owsley, *The American People: A History*

David L. Cohn, *Where I Was Born and Raised*

E. Merton Coulter, *Georgia: A Short History*

Jonathan Daniels, *A Southerner Discovers the South*

Donald Davidson, *Attack on Leviathan, Southern Writers in the Modern World*

Thomas DiLorenzo, *Hamilton's Curse*

John Emison, *The Martin Luther King Congressional Cover-Up*

Thomas Fleming, *The Politics of Human Nature, The Morality of Everyday Life*

John Gould Fletcher, *Arkansas*

Samuel T. Francis, *Shots Fired, Leviathan and Its Enemies*

Richard Gamble, *A Fiery Gospel, In Search of the City on a Hill, War for Righteousness*

George Garrett, *My Silk Purse and Yours, Whistling in the Dark, Poison Pen*

Eugene Genovese, *The Southern Front, The Southern Tradition*

Caroline Gordon, *Collected Stories*

Zane Grey, *The Zane Grey Frontier Trilogy*

Michael Andrew Grissom, *When the South Was Southern, The Last Rebel Yell*

DuBose Heyward, *Porgy and Bess, Carolina Chansons*

Jay B. Hubbell, *The South in American Literature*

Zora Neale Hurston, *Dust Tracks on a Road, Mules and Men*

Randall Ivey, *The Shape of a Man*

Caryl Johnston, *Stewards of History*

Harnett T. Kane, *The Bayous of Louisiana*

Florence King, *Reflections in a Jaundiced Eye, Stet! Dammit, Deja Reviews*

Lloyd E. Lenard, *The Last Confederate Flag*

Donald Livingston, ed., *Rethinking the American Union, Philosophical Delirium and Melancholy*

Brion McClanahan, *The Founding Fathers' Constitution, Forgotten Conservatives in American History* (with Clyde N. Wilson)

William March, *Company K*

John Marquardt, *Eighty Years Around the World*

Harriett C. Owsley, ed., *Frank Lawrence Owsley: Historian of the Old South*

Walker Percy, *The Thanatos Syndrome*

William Alexander Percy, *Lanterns on the Levee*

Julia Peterkin, *Scarlet Sister Mary*

William S. Powell, *North Carolina: A History*

Charles P. Roland, *The Improbable Era*

Louis D. Rubin, Jr., and James J. Kilpatrick, eds., *The Lasting South*

Archibald Rutledge, *Life's Extras, My Colonel and His Lady*

Franklin Sanders, *Heiland, A Home in Dogwood Mudhole*

Joseph Scotchie, *Revolt from the Heartland, Writing on the Southern Front, Barbarians in the Saddle, A Gallery of Ashevillians*

Francis B. Simkins and Charles P. Roland, *A History of the South*

Elliott White Springs, *War Birds: The Diary of an Unknown Aviator*

H.V. Traywick, Jr., *Starlight on the Rails*

Leslie Tucker, *Old Times There Should Not Be Forgotten*

John Vinson, *Southerner, Take Your Stand!*

Robert Penn Warren, *The Legacy of the Civil War*, *The Collected Poems*

Richard M. Weaver, *Visions of Order*, *In Defense of Tradition*

Walter Prescott Webb, *Divided We Stand*

Howard R. White, *The C.S.A. Trilogy*

Ellen Williams, *Bedford: A World Vision*

Clyde N. Wilson, *Defending Dixie*, *From Union to Empire*, Ed., *Why the South Will Survive*, *Annals of the Stupid Party*

Mark Royden Winchell, *Where No Flag Flies: Donald Davidson and the Southern Resistance*, *Ideas in Conflict* (with Donna P. Winchell), *God, Man, and Hollywood*

Thomas Wolfe, *O Lost!*

Tom Wolfe, *I Am Charlotte Simmons*, *A Man in Full*, *Back to Blood*

Raymond Wolters, *The Long Crusade*

About the Author

DR. CLYDE N. WILSON is Emeritus Distinguished Professor of History of the University of South Carolina, where he served from 1971 to 2006. He holds a Ph.D. from the University of North Carolina at Chapel Hill. Wilson was editor of the 28-volume edition of *The Papers of John C. Calhoun* which has received high praise. He is author or editor of more than 20 other books and over 700 articles, essays, and reviews in a variety of books and journals, and has lectured all over the U.S. and in Europe.

Dr. Wilson directed 17 doctoral dissertations, a number of which have been published. Books written or edited include *Why the South Will Survive, Carolina Cavalier: The Life and Mind of James Johnston Pettigrew, The Essential Calhoun*, three volumes of *The Dictionary of Literary Biography* on American Historians, *From Union to Empire: Essays in the Jeffersonian Tradition, Defending Dixie: Essays in Southern History and Culture, Chronicles of the South*, and *The Yankee Problem*.

Dr. Wilson is founding director of the Society of Independent Southern Historians; former president of the St. George Tucker Society for Southern Studies; recipient of the Bostick Prize for Contributions to South Carolina Letters, the first annual John Randolph Society Lifetime Achievement Award, and of the Robert E. Lee Medal of the Sons of Confederate Veterans. He is M.E. Bradford

Distinguished Professor of the Abbeville Institute; former Contributing Editor of *Chronicles: A Magazine of American Culture*; founding dean of the Stephen D. Lee Institute, educational arm of the Sons of Confederate Veterans; and co-founder of Shotwell Publishing.

Dr. Wilson has two grown daughters, an excellent son-in-law, and two outstanding grandsons. He lives in the Dutch Fork of South Carolina, not far from the Santee Swamp where Francis Marion and his men rested between raids on the first invader.

Available from Shotwell Publishing

IF YOU ENJOYED THIS BOOK, perhaps some of our other titles will pique your interest. The following titles are currently available from Shotwell at most major online book retailers.

MARK C. ATKINS
- *Women in Combat: Feminism Goes to War*

JOYCE BENNETT
- *Maryland, My Maryland: The Cultural Cleansing of a Small Southern State*

GARRY BOWERS
- *Slavery and the Civil War: What Your History Teacher Didn't Tell You*
- *Dixie Days: Reminiscences of a Southern Boyhood*

JERRY BREWER
- *Dismantling the Republic*

ANDREW P. CALHOUN, JR.
- *My Own Darling Wife: Letters From a Confederate Volunteer [John Francis Calhoun]*

JOHN CHODES
- *Segregation: Federal Policy or Racism?*
- *Washington's KKK: The Union League During Southern Reconstruction*

PAUL C. GRAHAM
- *Confederaphobia: An American Epidemic*

(Free eBook version available at ShotwellPublishing.com)

- *When the Yankees Come: Former South Carolina Slaves Remember Sherman's Invasion*

JOSEPH JAY
- *Sacred Conviction: The South's Stand for Biblical Authority*

SUZANNE PARFITT JOHNSON
- *Maxcy Gregg's Sporting Journal 1842 - 1858*

JAMES R. KENNEDY
- *Dixie Rising: Rules for Rebels*
- *When Rebel Was Cool*

JAMES R. KENNEDY & WALTER D. KENNEDY
- *Punished with Poverty: The Suffering South*
- *Yankee Empire: Aggressive Abroad and Despotic At Home*
- *The South Was Right! A New Edition for the 21st Century*

PHILIP LEIGH
- *The Devil's Town: Hot Spring During the Gangster Era*
- *U.S. Grant's Failed Presidency*
- *Causes of the Civil War*

LEWIS LIBERMAN
X • *Snowflake Buddies: ABCs for Leftists*

JOHN MARQUARDT
- *Around the World in Eighty Years: Confessions of a Connecticut Confederate*

MICHAEL MARTIN
- *Southern Grit: Sensing the Siege at Petersburg*

SAMUEL W. MITCHAM
- *The Greatest Lynching in American History: New York, 1863*

CHARLES T. PACE
- *Lincoln As He Really Was*
- *Southern Independence. Why War?*

JAMES RUTLEDGE ROESCH
- *From Founding Fathers to Fire Eaters: The Constitutional Doctrine of States' Rights in the Old South*

KIRKPATRICK SALE
- *Emancipation Hell: The Tragedy Wrought By Lincoln's Emancipation Proclamation*

ANNE WILSON SMITH
- *Robert E. Lee: A History Book for Kids*

KAREN STOKES
- *A Legion of Devils: Sherman in South Carolina*
- *Carolina Love Letters*

LESLIE R. TUCKER
- *Old Time There Should Not Be Forgotten: Cultural Genocide in Dixie*

JOHN VINSON
- *Southerner, Take Your Stand!*

HOWARD RAY WHITE
- *Understanding Creation and Evolution*
- *How Southern Families Made America*

CLYDE N. WILSON
- *Lies My Teacher Told Me: The True History of the War for Southern Independence & Other Essays*

(Free eBook version available at ShotwellPublishing.com)

- *The Old South: 50 Essential Books*

(Southern Reader's Guide I)

- *The War Between the States: 60 Essential Books*

(Southern Reader's Guide II)
- *Reconstruction and the New South: 50 Essential Books* (Southern Reader's Guide III)
- *The South – 20th Century and Beyond 50 Essential Books* (Southern Reader's Guide IV)

- *The Yankee Problem: An American Dilemma* (The Wilson Files 1)
- *Nullification: Reclaiming Consent of the Governed* (The Wilson Files 2)
- *Annals of the Stupid Party: Republicans Before Trump* (The Wilson Files 3)

JOE A. WOLVERTON, II
- *What Degree of Madness?" Madison's Method for Making American STATES Again*

WALTER KIRK WOOD
- *Beyond Slavery: The Northern Romantic Nationalist Origins of America's Civil War*

GREEN ALTAR BOOKS (Literary Imprint)

CATHARINE SAVAGE BROSMAN
- *An Aesthetic Education and Other Stories*
- *Chained Tree, Chained Owls: Poems*

RANDALL IVEY
- *A New England Romance & Other SOUTHERN Stories*

JAMES EVERETT KIBLER
- *Tiller* (Clay Bank County, IV)

KAREN STOKES
- *Belles: A Carolina Romance*
- *Honor in the Dust*
- *The Immortals*
- *The Soldier's Ghost: A Tale of Charleston*
- *Carolina Twilight*

WILLIAM A, THOMAS, JR.
- *Runaway Haley: An Imagined Family Saga*

GOLD-BUG (Mystery & Suspense Imprint)

MICHAEL ANDREW GRISSOM
- *Billie Jo: A Novel*

BRANDI PERRY
- *Splintered: A New Orleans Tale*

MARTIN L. WILSON
- *To Jekyll and Hide*

Free Book Offer

SIGN-UP FOR NEW RELEASE notifications and receive a FREE downloadable edition of *Lies My Teacher Told Me: The True History of the War for Southern Independence & Other Essays* by Dr. Clyde N. Wilson AND *Confederaphobia: An American Epidemic* by Paul C. Graham by visiting our website at ShotwellPublishing.com.

You can always unsubscribe and keep the book, so you've got nothing to lose!

SOUTHERN WITHOUT APOLOGY

www.ingramcontent.com/pod-product-compliance
Lightning Source LLC
Chambersburg PA
CBHW072016060426
42446CB00043B/2570